DEFEND
UNTIL DEATH!

NICKOLAS FLUX and the Battle of the Alamo

BY Nel Yomtov

Graphic Library is published by Capstone Press,
1710 Roe Crest Drive, North Mankato, Minnesota 56003
www.capstonepub.com

Library of Congress Cataloging-in-Publication Data
Yomtov, Nelson.
  Defend until death! : Nickolas Flux and the Battle of the Alamo / by
Nel Yomtov ; illustrated by Dante Ginevra.
    pages cm.—(Graphic library. Nickolas Flux history chronicles)
  Summary: "In graphic novel format, follows the adventures of
Nickolas Flux as he travels back in time and must survive the Battle
of the Alamo"—Provided by publisher.
  Includes bibliographical references and index.
  ISBN 978-1-4765-3945-4 (library binding)
  ISBN 978-1-4765-5149-4 (paperback)
  ISBN 978-1-4765-6006-9 (eBook PDF)
1. Alamo (San Antonio, Tex.)—Juvenile literature. 2. Alamo (San An-
tonio, Tex.)—Siege, 1836—Juvenile literature. 3. Texas—History—To
1846—Juvenile literature. 4. San Antonio (Tex.)—Buildings, structures,
etc.—Juvenile literature. 5. Alamo (San Antonio, Tex.)—Comic books,
strips, etc. 6. Alamo (San Antonio, Tex.)—Siege, 1836—Comic books,
strips, etc. 7. Texas—History—To 1846—Comic books, strips, etc. 8.
San Antonio (Tex.)—Buildings, structures, etc.—Comic books, strips, etc.
I. Ginevra, Dante, 1976– illustrator. II. Title.
  F390.Y66 2014
  976.4'03—dc23   2013028000

Photo Credits:
Design Elements: Shutterstock (backgrounds)

Editor's note:
A direct quotation appears on the following page:
Page 17 (letter), from a letter by William Travis dated February 24,
1836, taken from the Texas State Library and Archives Commission
(http://www.tsl.state.tx.us/treasures/republic/alamo/travis-about.html).

EDITOR
Christopher L. Harbo

DESIGNER
Ashlee Suker

ART DIRECTOR
Nathan Gassman

PRODUCTION SPECIALIST
Kathy McColley

Printed in the United States of America in Stevens Point, Wisconsin.
092013   007767WZS14

TABLE OF CONTENTS

FLUX FACT

Santa Anna's march included more than 4,000 men, 21 field cannon, 1,800 mules, and hundreds of wagons loaded with food and supplies.

FLUX FACT

In December 1821, Stephen Austin led the first American colonists into Texas territory. By 1824, 300 American families, known as Texians, had settled in Texas.

FLUX FACT

Antonio López de Santa Anna served as president of Mexico 11 times between 1833 and 1855. He was overthrown each time.

CHAPTER THREE

PREPARING TO FIGHT

February 23, 1836, the outskirts of San Antonio

The townspeople have spotted our scouts, general. They have abandoned the town and fled into the Alamo compound.

Excellent! We will crush this rebellion ...

... starting now!

He plans on killing everyone defending the mission.

The Texians already know they're in danger.

But I've got to warn them that Santa Anna will not let them surrender.

south entrance to the Alamo

I'm doomed if the Texians think I'm with the Mexican Army ...

Halt!

FLUX FACT

Jim Bowie was an American soldier and pioneer known for the large knife he carried. He came to the Alamo to fight. But a serious illness kept him in bed in the low barracks.

Take the letter to my messenger. Tell him to deliver it to other American fighters in nearby forts.

Yes, sir.

FLUX FACT

Travis' letter reached other Texian rebels. But a relief expedition of 300 men and supplies broke down on its way from the nearby town of Goliad. The expedition never made it to the Alamo.

FLUX FACT

According to legend, Travis drew a line in the sand as he spoke to his men on March 5. He asked anyone who would stay and fight to cross the line and join him. Every man—except one—crossed the line.

ATTACK!

Nick, I'll defend the north wall. Go help Crockett at the south wall.

I'm on my way, sir.

I'm here to help, Davy. What can I do?

We've turned them back here, Nick. Run and inform Lieutenant Colonel Travis.

I'll be right back.

FLUX FACT

The Mexican attackers were packed so tightly together that some of them accidentally shot their fellow soldiers. More Mexicans were killed by "friendly fire" than by the Texian rebels.

FLUX FACT

Davy Crockett was killed in the fighting. To this day no one is certain how he died. Some historians claim he was killed in the barracks. Others believe he surrendered and was executed after the fighting ended.

FLUX FACT

Santa Anna ordered his soldiers to take no prisoners. However, the general did spare all the women and children at the Alamo. About 20 were allowed to return to their homes.

CHAPTER FIVE

BATTLES LOST AND WON

Present day, 8:48 p.m.

TOUCHDOWN!

Nick, where have you been? You missed half the game.

And you're covered in dirt.

Oh ... yeah ... well ... I tripped on the way back from the concession stand.

Well, you missed quite a battle.

That's what you think.

While Wes and Myra watched this game, I saw the Alamo fall.

FLUX FILES

TEXAS TERRITORY

Mexico won its independence from Spain in 1821. Texas became a territory within the new nation of Mexico. Texas was one-third the size of the United States at that time.

SPANISH MISSION

The Alamo was originally called San Antonio de Valero. It was a mission built by the Spanish government and used by the Catholic Church. In about 1803, it became a fortress for the Mexican Army. The word alamo means "cottonwood tree" in Spanish.

FIGHTING FOR INDEPENDENCE

Texian settlers believed the Mexican government's policies were harsh toward them. In 1830, the government passed laws to stop American immigration into Texas. In 1833, Santa Anna denied the settlers' request to establish an independent state in Mexico. Doing so would have allowed the settlers to make their own laws and govern themselves. The settlers' anger eventually lead to armed revolts against the Mexicans.

THE ALAMO SIEGE

Santa Anna's siege of the Alamo lasted 12 days before the final attack. During that time, his army fired about 200 cannonballs into the compound. Not one Texian was injured in the constant shelling.

COWARD OF THE ALAMO

Only one man fled the mission when Lieutenant Colonel Travis asked his men to stay and fight on March 5. Louis "Moses" Rose was later nicknamed the "Coward of the Alamo."

JIM BOWIE

Jim Bowie was killed in his bed. Many historians agree that he died after emptying his pistols into several Mexican soldiers.

LIVES LOST

No one knows the exact number of people who died at the Battle of the Alamo. The Alamo's official list counts 189 defenders who lost their lives. Historians estimate about 600 Mexican soldiers died during the battle.

REMEMBER THE ALAMO!

Seven weeks after the fall of the Alamo, an army of rebels defeated Mexican troops at the Battle of San Jacinto. Rallying with cries of "Remember the Alamo!" the Texians killed about 650 Mexicans and captured Santa Anna. Texas became an independent state. In 1845, Texas joined the United States as its 28th state.

GLOSSARY

BARRACKS (BAR-uhks) — the part of a fort where soldiers sleep

COMPOUND (KAHM-paund) — a group of buildings often enclosed by a fence or wall

EXPEDITION (ek-spuh-DISH-uhn) — a journey made for a specific purpose

FORT (FORT) — a building that is well defended against attacks

FORTIFIED (FOR-tuh-fyed) — having had walls built for protection from attack

FRONTIER (fruhn-TEER) — the far edge of a settled area, where few people live

MISSION (MISH-uhn) — a church or other place where missionaries live and work

PIONEER (pye-uh-NEER) — someone who moves to live in a new land

REBEL (REB-uhl) — a person who opposes a government or ruler

SHARPSHOOTER (SHARP-shoo-tur) — someone skilled at hitting small or distant targets

SIEGE (SEEJ) — an attack designed to surround a place and cut it off from supplies and help

SURRENDER (suh-REN-dur) — to give up or admit defeat

READ MORE

JEFFREY, GARY. *The Battle of the Alamo.* A Graphic History of the American West. New York. Gareth Stevens Pub., 2012.

LANDAU, ELAINE. *The Alamo: Would You Join the Fight?* What Would You Do? Berkeley Heights, N.J.: Enslow Publishers Inc., 2014.

SOUTH, VICTOR. *Remember the Alamo: Americans Fight for Texas, 1820–1845.* How America Became America. Philadelphia: Mason Crest Publishers, 2013.

INTERNET SITES

FactHound offers a safe, fun way to find Internet sites related to this book. All sites on FactHound have been researched by our staff.

Here's all you do:

Visit *www.facthound.com*

Type in this code: 9781476539454

Super-cool stuff!

Check out projects, games and lots more at
www.capstonekids.com

ABOUT THE AUTHOR

Nel Yomtov is a writer of children's nonfiction books and graphic novels. He specializes in writing about history, country studies, science, and biography. His graphic novel adaptation, *Jason and the Golden Fleece*, published by Stone Arch Books, was a winner of the 2009 Moonbeam Children's Book Award and the 2011 Lighthouse Literature Award. Nel is an avid American military history buff and has written two additional graphic novels for Capstone, *True Stories of World War I* and *True Stories of the Civil War*. He lives in the New York City area.